What Sport Do You Play?

Seed Learning

tennis

baseball

soccer

golf

basketball

volleyball

badminton

hockey

What sport do you play?

I play tennis.

What sport do you play?

I play baseball.

What sport do you play?

I play soccer.

What sport do you play?

I play golf.

What sport do you play?

I play basketball.

What sport do you play?

I play hockey.

Let's learn more about Thailand.

Tom yum